Behind the Wheel

Vanna White's Remarkable Story

George Hope Publishing

Contents

Biography

American television personality Vanna White is best known for presenting the game show "Wheel of Fortune" on "NBC." Despite having roles in numerous TV shows and movies, her work as the show's "letter-turner" is what made her famous and wealthy.

She has been able to captivate the audience with her beauty, charm, and energy since she started hosting the show. 'Vannamania' gripped the country for several years to the point where parents began naming their newborns after the celebrity.

Although the fascination has somewhat subsided, she is still highly well-liked and has established herself as a fashion icon. The 'Vanna' doll and perfume line are now hugely famous among her followers. She is a well-known television personality in addition to being a proud mother of two and a crocheter and knitter.

Her favourite activity is crocheting, which she learned to do from her grandma. Her crochet creations are frequently presented as gifts. 'Lion Brand Vanna's Choice Yarn' is the name of the yarn line she also created. Even so, she has written an autobiography titled "Vanna Speaks."

Early Life

On February 18, 1957, in North Myrtle Beach, South Carolina, Vanna Marie Rosich became Vanna White. When Vanna was a little child, her parents got divorced, and she was brought up in North Myrtle Beach by her mother Joan, and stepfather Herbert White Jr.

After high school, White relocated to Atlanta, Georgia, where she worked as a model and attended the Atlanta School of Fashion. She moved to Los Angeles in 1979 to pursue a career in acting, but she made a quick trip back to South Carolina in the summer of 1980 to visit her mother, who was passing away from ovarian cancer.

With newfound determination, White returned to Hollywood and landed a string of small acting roles in mostly forgettable films, including the part of Mickey in Gipsy Angels (1980), a cameo appearance with Albert Finney in Looker (1981), and the small role of Doris in the high school thriller Graduation Day (1981). In 1982, she also had an appearance in one episode of the TV show Star of the Family.

White, however, landed the position that would launch her career later in 1982. She was picked from among 200 candidates to work alongside new host and former weatherman Pat Sajak on the NBC game program Wheel of Fortune, which was developed by the legendary Merv Gryphon.

Over the following years, the program enjoyed enormous popularity; by 1986, a syndicated evening version had attracted 30 million viewers, double the audience of the No. 2 syndicated program, M*A*S*H, and was earning $100 million annually. About 40 million people watched Wheel of Fortune in 1999, the show's 16th year in syndication.

White soon rose to fame on Wheel of Fortune thanks to her roles as hostess, chief letter-turner, and model for an ever-evolving collection of outfits. "Vannamania" suddenly spread across the country, and White quickly amassed several lucrative endorsement deals and even landed the lead role in the NBC film Venus: The Goddess of Love. Although some media critics made fun of White for her poor acting skills and her role as a non-speaking clotheshorse on Wheel, the majority of viewers came to like her thanks in large part to her beauty, vivacity, and unfailing charisma.

As a result, White gained some notoriety in American popular culture. In the middle to late 1980s, she reached the height of her fame.

With an average of 720 claps in each episode and more than 28,000 in a season, White was recognized in The Guinness Book of World Records in 1992 as the most frequent clapper on television. In 1987, Vanna Speaks, a ghostwritten autobiography of the game show presenter, was released.

White has said of her long tenure on Wheel of Fortune, "It's not the most intellectual job in the world, but I do have to know the letters." Additionally, she once jokingly said, "When I was having that alphabet soup, I never thought that it would pay off."

When Sajak underwent emergency surgery at a hospital in late 2019, White, who had been hosting Wheel of Fortune for more than three decades, stepped in to take over. In the autumn of 2024, when Sajak is replaced as presenter by Ryan Seacrest, White will still be a part of the program.

White requested a pay increase as her contract came to an end in the 2023–24 season because it had been 18 years since she had gotten one for the syndicated version of Wheel of Fortune. To obtain a pay rise, White recruited the well-known and tenacious entertainment attorney Bryan Freedman.

Despite having previously earned pay increases for the ABC version of the show, Celebrity Wheel of Fortune, she was reportedly earning $3 million annually for the syndicated version of the program, which is over five times Sajak's salary. On September 19, 2023, it was revealed that White had signed a challenging two-year contract extension. Although the contract's specifics were kept private, TMZ said that White earned a "substantial pay increase."

Personal Life

In 1986, tragedy struck White's personal life when her longtime partner, John Gibson, a soap opera actor and Chippendales dancer, perished in an aircraft crash.

White wed restaurateur George San Pietro in 1990. Their daughter Giovanna was born in 1997, and their son Nicholas was born in 1994. In 2002, White and San Pietro were divorced. She became engaged to financier Michael Kaye a few years later, but they never wed. Later, White started a committed relationship with property developer John Donaldson.

Career, Major works and Legacy

Vanna White moved back to Los Angeles after her mother's passing and carried on her waitressing job there. In the meanwhile, she was able to secure tiny parts in films like "Looker" (1981) and "Graduation Day" (1981).

Vanna made an appearance in a "Star of the Family" episode from 1982. She participated in a "Wheel of Fortune" audition later in November and was selected from 200 candidates to appear on the game show as a co-host and letter-turner.

On December 13th, 1982, Vanna joined the 'Wheel of Fortune' for the first time. She has been serving as the daytime hostess of the program ever since. Additionally, she co-hosts the nighttime edition of the program with Pat Sajak.

Vanna White's fame started to rise when a syndicated episode of "Wheel of Fortune" aired in September 1983. The program attracted 30 million viewers and made $100 million by 1986. There were 40 million viewers by the year 1999.

Vanna released her autobiography, "Vanna Speaks," in May 1987. Her enormous popularity helped the book become a smash seller.

Vanna portrayed Venus in the 1988 film "Goddess of Love" in which she made an appearance. A television movie called "Goddess of Love" aired on "NBC." Unfortunately, her performance failed to get praise. She further made an appearance as a guest timekeeper at "WrestleMania IV" that same year.

Vanna provided notable character voices for two animated TV shows in the 1990s. The Real Story of Twinkle, Twinkle Little Star, a 1992 Canadian animated television special, and Captain Planet and the Planeteers, an American animated television series that aired from 1990 to 1996, respectively, were the two examples.

She had a brief cameo appearance in the third and last "Naked Gun" movie, "Naked Gun 3313: The Final Insult," released in 1994. She was hired to perform and serve as the primary narrator for the 1996 CD edition of "Santa's Last Ride."

Later on, she appeared in several series as a cameo, including "L.A. Law," "227," "Super Mario Bros. Super Show," "Simon and Simon," "The King of

Queens," and "Full House." She additionally had a cameo appearance on "Married...With Children." She had a cameo appearance in "Fresh Off the Boat" in 2017.

On December 13, 1982, Vanna White made her 'Wheel of Fortune' debut. She has continued to frequently host the program ever since. She became a household name in the US after appearing on "Wheel of Fortune," which elevated her fame.

Every year, Vanna gives St. Jude's Research Hospital a portion of the sales revenue from her "Lion Brand Vanna's Choice Yarn."

Vanna White began dating actor-turned-dancer John Gibson in 1980. Sadly, John lost his life in an aircraft accident in 1986. Vanna had to take a break from the program since it was such a major blow to her.

On December 31, 1990, Vanna wed restaurateur George Santo Pietro. Twelve years later, the couple were divorced. From this union, she has two children: Nicholas (born in 1994) and Giovanna (born in 1997).
Vanna became engaged to Michael Kaye, a significant corporate figure in southern California,

in 2004. They never wed, though, and the engagement was called off in 2006.

At one point, Vanna was so well-liked that the term "Vannamania" was created to describe the adoration her millions of followers had for her.

In April 2006, she was awarded a star on the "Hollywood Walk of Fame."

Vanna White was included as "television's most frequent clapper" in the "Guinness Book of World Records" in 1992. It is estimated that she claps 600 times every performance.

Relationship History

Vanna has only had one marriage. From 1990 until 2002, she was married to George and Vanna. For his appearances in For All Mankind, The Mandalorian, and Alias, former restaurateur and actor George Santo is most known. The ex-couple disclosed they were expecting a child in 1992 during the Wheel of Fortune puzzle, despite the TV celebrity remaining mute about the relationship at the time.

They tragically lost the child. The spouse of the former Vanna White supported her up until the birth of their son Nicholas Santo Pietro in 1995. Two years later, they gave birth to Gigi Santo Pietro, a daughter. However, on May 15, 2002, the former couple filed for divorce after 12 years of marriage.

Over the years, the TV personality has had romantic relationships with famous people. The breakdown of Vanna White's relationships is shown below.

(1982 - 1986) John Gibson

In the 1980s, she became engaged to actor and dancer John Gibson. The Young and the Restless episode where the American actor played Cash Cashman made him famous. Following his death in an aircraft crash in Los Angeles in 1982, Gibson and the co-host of Wheel of Fortune dated until 1986.

(2004–2006) Michael Kaye

White's marriage to George dissolved, and in 2004 she became engaged to Southern California businessman Michael Kaye. Up to their breakup in 2006, the couple remained together. Donaldson, John

(2012-Present)

After that, she started dating John Donaldson. Thanks to their shared friends, the two connected in 2012. Donaldson, who owns JDC Construction + Development Group, is a successful contractor despite not being a Hollywood star. Since 1992, the business has expanded to work with some of Hollywood's biggest names, such as Martin Mull, Dan Akroyd, and Richard Dreyfuss.

There has long been a perception that Pat Sajak and Vanna are dating. They began appearing on the venerable game program Wheel of Fortune in the early 1980s and developed a strong relationship over time. The two always get along on television, and many have remarked on what a beautiful couple they would make. It took the two a few years to persuade folks that their previous April Fool's joke about being in a relationship was just that. In actuality, their friendship continues long after the program, and their connection is solely professional.

The proud mother of two is an American TV personality. With her ex-husband George Santo Pietro, she gave birth to her children Nicholas Pietro (Niko) and Giovanna Pietro (Gigi). All of Vanna White's children are now adults. Given that Nicholas Pietro was born on June 10, 1994, he will be 29 years old in 2023. He is a cook with experience, a TV personality, and is presently learning about art.

The only daughter and second child, Giovanna Pietro, is presently 25 years old and a tattoo artist in Los Angeles.

The Stunning Transformation Of Vanna White

For many years, Vanna White has graced television screens throughout the country. If you only say "Vanna," everyone will know who you are referring to.

After all, she is renowned for rotating the letters on the Wheel of Fortune puzzle board. It was unknown when Pat Sajak picked the young, fresh-faced South Carolina native to join him as a co-host on Wheel of Fortune, but it's now difficult to picture the famous game show without her.

White is well aware of how peculiar her job description is since she has built a career out of knowing the alphabet. White once said, according to Biography, "I never thought that it would pay off when I was having that alphabet soup." She became well-known as a result of her appearance on the show, and she has since had a happy life.

But there are many things about Vanna White that you probably don't know. How then did White become so recognizable? How did she live before making her Wheel of Fortune debut? Take a peek at Vanna White's amazing transformation.

Vanna Marie Rosich, her given name at birth, was who she was before becoming Vanna White. White was reared at North Myrtle Beach after being born in South Carolina in 1957. White told Grand Strand magazine, "Growing up in a tiny community like North Myrtle Beach was fantastic and to my favour.

I brought that small-town girl to Hollywood with the same ideals, and I still don't feel all that different.

White has Latin ancestry because her grandparents are from Spain and her father was born in Cuba. According to Biography, her parents separated when she was a baby, and her father fled before she was even born. White's mother and stepfather, Herbert White Jr., who formally adopted her when she was 3 years old, reared her instead.

White didn't find out Herbert wasn't her real father until she was 12 years old. White, meanwhile, doesn't appear to have seen any difference. Later, she admitted that Herbert, her stepfather, was her biological father on Larry King Live. He has been raising me since I was three.

Vanna White relocated to Atlanta, Georgia, after finishing high school to attend college there.

According to CBS Sunday Morning, she enrolled and attended the Atlanta School for Fashion and Design where she learned poise and fashion merchandising with the ultimate objective of becoming a professional model. Since a large part of White's position on Wheel of Fortune requires her to look poised on camera, it's a good thing that she went to college.

White decided to leave the East Coast and move to Hollywood after completing college in Atlanta. Like the majority of recent college grads, she had few resources. "I had $1,000 to my name — $300 for the car, $700 for the flat, and a job immediately... waitressing," White revealed in a CBS Sunday Morning interview.

On the west coast, White's entry into the world of professional modelling would prove challenging, as she battled to get work in Los Angeles much like many others do. "I couldn't pay the rent, and I was too proud to ask my dad for rent money," White said in her Biography. Therefore, I took some lingerie photos.

Vanna White competed in the Miss Georgia USA beauty contest in 1978 before relocating from the East Coast to begin her new life in Los Angeles. She would have competed in the Miss USA competition as the competitor representing Georgia if she had won the pageant. The host revealed throughout the pageant that she enjoyed playing the guitar and piano. White stated during the pageant, "I'm a professional model, and I'd like to further my career in this industry. And I love meeting new people," she continued.

White, who competed in the swimsuit category wearing a blue one-piece, said she was "very excited" when told she may be travelling to the Miss USA pageant. According to TV Guide, White placed as the fourth runner-up since it was not intended to be. What might've been!

Vanna White decided to move to Los Angeles in her early 20s, but she was unable to stay there for very long. White learned her mother was gravely ill soon after landing in Los Angeles. According to Grand Strand magazine, she had ovarian cancer and her prognosis was not good. Ovarian cancer signs might be hard to notice.

White said as much in a Larry King Live interview, "It was very tough." "I returned home. I took care of the issue before returning to this area, ready to attack. White answered "Absolutely" when asked if losing her mother was the "toughest loss of all."

White and her mother have a strong relationship, and with all of her accomplishments, she has never forgotten her. "Joan, my mother, was the greatest mother ever! I adore you a thousand times over! On Mother's Day 2015, White said on Instagram, "You will always be with me in spirit.

Vanna White originally debuted on a popular daytime TV game show before becoming a nightly staple on our television screens. White took part in The Price Is Right in 1980. At the time, she was 23 years old and a recent immigrant to Los Angeles.

White's appearance on The Price Is Right unfortunately wasn't particularly productive. Except for those nice leaving presents, I didn't win a doggone thing, White said to Yahoo Superfan in 2016.

Her debut on the game show will be best remembered for the moment Bob Barker called her out. She kept glancing at herself on the monitor, so he warned her that she probably wasn't doing very well with her pricing predictions. White, on the other hand, had a different account to share. I was glancing towards my pal in hopes of getting a response from her. Informed Yahoo Superfan, White. All I could think was, "It just looked like I was looking at the monitor."

Early in the 1980s, when she was hired as the co-host of Wheel of Fortune, Vanna White had her big break in the entertainment industry. White competed in an audition among 200 other female candidates to fill Susan Stafford's former co-host position. White's selection as the new co-host was eventually made by the show's originator, Merv Gryphon.

In reality, Pat Sajak didn't suggest White, and he later claimed that he had advised Gryphon not to choose her. She was the most anxious of all of them, Sajak said, "not that she wasn't lovely and wonderful and personable and all that, but she was the most nervous of any of them." Gryphon disregarded Sajak's advice, and the rest is history, as they say.

Wheel of Fortune has been co-hosted by White and Sajak for many years. White made her game show debut shortly after "Vanna-mania" swept the country. The stunning woman twisting the letters while beaming broadly captured the attention of the

American people. White said, "That was when I was in the grocery queue checking out, and I was on the cover of Newsweek," when questioned by CBS Sunday Morning about the moment she realised she had achieved success. Wow, I think I've made it, I thought.

Several years after beginning her career on Wheel of Fortune, in 1986, Vanna White learned terrible news about her fiancé. She was engaged to Chippendales dancer and actor John Gibson from The Young and the Restless. According to the Los Angeles Times, Gibson tragically perished when the aircraft he was piloting went down in the San Fernando Valley, close to the Van Nuys airport.

Naturally, the news upset White. When this horrible event occurred, I was in the height of Vanna-mania, White said to Closer Weekly. "My fans' unwavering support made me feel like I wasn't alone," the author said.

America shared White's sorrow during this trying period and did their best to help the game show co-host. "I heard from so many people who had shared the same experience of losing someone instantly in an accident, and that helped me," White said in an individual interview. I didn't believe I was alone.

Vanna White had both a career peak and a career low in 1987. As reported by the Chicago Tribune, she published her autobiography under the title Vanna Speaks. The ironic name made fun of her largely quiet performance on the well-known TV game program.

White's book release, nevertheless, was overshadowed by more important news. Vanna White was featured on the cover of Playboy magazine's May edition of that year (according to The Washington Post), shocking the nation.

White had shot obscene lingerie photographs to pay her rent when she had first moved to Los Angeles. Hugh Hefner of Playboy acquired those images, and he used them both as a spread and the cover of his publication (according to Time). "He is the one who chose to feature me on the magazine's cover. For Playboy, I didn't do it," White told Fox News.

Fortunately, White was left alone by the Wheel of Fortune network, as she told Fox News: "I was very thankful that I had such support behind me." The embarrassing photos taken by White were quickly forgotten and forgiven by the American public.

Vanna White married restaurateur George Santo Pietro in 1988 after the tragic death of her engaged partner in 1986. In 1992, the couple made happy news, and White naturally used her day job to make it enjoyable to share with the public.

According to the Los Angeles Times, a participant in a 1992 edition of Wheel of Fortune correctly answered a riddle with the phrase "VANNA'S PREGNANT." Although she wonderfully announced the news, it was regrettably too soon.

White miscarried shortly after that. In an interview with Closer Weekly, White revealed, "I was so ready to be a mother." I'm not sure how to put into words that loss. White recalled the advice her mother had given her in the wake of such tragedy. Never give up, under any circumstances," White recalled. "Follow your dreams and your emotions. And I carried it out.

It's understandable to assume that Vanna White would lose her desire to continue trying to grow her family after experiencing so many heartbreaking losses. Her miscarriage, the passing of her fiancé, and the deaths of her mother did not, however, cause her to lose heart. She gave birth to a healthy baby boy named Nicholas, also known as Nikko, in 1994 with the help of her husband, George Santo Pietro. According to Closer Weekly, White gave birth to a daughter called Giovanna, also known as Gigi, a few years later.

White had finally realised her ambition of having two children by the time she and Pietro formed their family of four. White told Closer Weekly, "We're faced with a lot of positives and negatives, and we have to accept them and do what we can to get through it." Life is not perfect, so just try to make the most of it, she continued. Be courageous, considerate, and joyful.

Sadly, White and Pietro eventually got divorced. According to Closer Weekly, White would settle into a relationship with contractor John Donaldson following an engagement and separation with businessman Michael Kaye.

Vanna White said that receiving a star on the Hollywood Walk of Fame was her greatest success when Larry King questioned her about the "proudest accomplishment" of her career during a part on Larry King Now. Being honoured in the entertainment industry is not something that everyone receives, therefore it makes sense to be proud of it. After participating in Wheel of Fortune for more than 20 years, White was awarded a star in April 2006.

"At the age of 10, I recall my parents telling me, 'You can accomplish anything you want.' Dad, we succeeded. According to the Herald Tribune, White stated during the event honouring the unveiling of her star on the Hollywood Walk of Fame.

When White received her star, which was the 2,309th on the Walk of Fame, she was joined by her father, her co-host Pat Sajak, Wheel of Fortune founder Merv Gryphon, and Jeopardy! presenter Alex Trebek.

Following a 1986 appearance on The Tonight Show with Johnny Carson with Joan Rivers as a special guest, Vanna White spoke about her love of crocheting and later became a spokeswoman for Lion Brand Yarn. Her proficiency in crochet increased even further when, in 2007, she collaborated with Lion Brand Yarn to develop her line, "Vanna's Choice."

When White was five years old, her grandmother taught her how to crochet for the very first time. Years later, White observed her hairstylist crocheting on the set of Wheel of Fortune. After receiving a refresher from her hairstylist, White started up the activity once more.

She later taught her daughter how to crochet as well. "I crochet whenever I have free time on the set. In an interview with Etsy, White stated, "I find it to be calming, and I have something to show for the time I've spent on it.

Half of White's yarn sales are donated. She gave more than $1,700,000 to St. Jude Children's Research Hospital by the year 2016.

Vanna White was given a tremendous honour in 2013. She now holds the record for the most frequent clapper in history. Kimberly Patrick, a representative from the Guinness Book of World Records, handed White the record certificate on a May 2013 episode of Wheel of Fortune. It was an honour to offer Vanna White this record and thank her for her support of competitors throughout 30 seasons of Wheel of Fortune, Patrick added.

According to Guinness, White had applauded 3,480,864 times during 30 seasons of Wheel of Fortune as of January 31, 2013. The 606 claps per episode average was used to get this number. That's a lot of applause, and White was honoured for the incredible feat as the show was being filmed.

After 30 years of recording the TV game show, White's record of more than 3 million claps was attained in 2013, thus the figure is undoubtedly much greater now.

On Wheel of Fortune, Vanna White is renowned for her outfit. Every edition of the game show has the co-host decked up in a stunning dress and high heels. The fact that White has never worn the same dress twice in more than 35 years of shooting is extremely astounding, as White revealed on The Wendy Williams Show.

White's outfits never fail to astound and inspire. Around 6,500 gowns were said to have been worn by her as of 2017, and as the show goes on, that total only keeps going up.

According to ABC News, White tried on a minimum of 50 gowns before deciding which ones she would wear for the presentation. White needs around ten minutes to change clothes between show tapings because Wheel of Fortune records six programs in a single day (per Good Housekeeping).

Despite not being permitted to retain the gowns, White has developed a few favourites over the years from donning so many different looks. It appears that she chooses her favourites based on their usefulness. White told ABC News, "I prefer wearing the short ones most. Simply because I don't fall.

10 Things You Might Not Know About Wheel of Fortune Star Vanna White

For more than 40 years, Vanna White has been releasing letters on the Wheel of Fortune puzzle board, and in 2019, she even served as the show's host. But up until this point, she has never tried her luck as a contender.

On Wednesday, White, 66, will spin and solve as part of a unique "Ultimate Host Night" edition of Wheel. She will be on Jeopardy as we guess letters! Mayim Bialik and Ken Jennings are the emcees, and all proceeds benefit charity.

White, who took over for model Susan Stafford as the show's full-time letter-turner in 1982, has been waiting more than 40 years for this exceptional occasion. Her success sparked a surge of "Vannamania," and she and Wheel presenter Pat Sajak went on to establish themselves as one of the most recognizable television teams of all time.

Here are some interesting facts about White, a native of North Myrtle Beach, South Carolina, in honour of his driving debut.

1. Vanna Marie Rosich was born on February 18, 1957, to parents Joan Marie and Miguel Angel Rosich. She was adopted by her stepfather. When White was only a few months old, her father abandoned her. She was adopted by her stepfather, Herbert Stackley White Jr., when she was 2 years old, and now goes by that name.

Throughout Vanna's professional life and until his passing on April 1, 2022, the two remained close. On an episode of Wheel from the year 2021, she said that she phoned him "every morning to say good morning and that I love you."

2. Before Wheel, she was a struggling performer.

Before getting her big break on Wheel, White was a struggling performer. After graduating from the Atlanta School of Fashion in 1979, she originally relocated to Los Angeles, but in 1980 she went back to be with her mother, who would shortly pass away from ovarian cancer.

White had a few small appearances in films including Graduation Day (1981) and Gipsy Angels, which wouldn't be released until years later in 1990, after moving back to Los Angeles. She admitted to sleeping on her apartment's floor once since she didn't have a bed, the Associated Press in 1986, even though she wasn't making a lot of money at the time. She also waited tables and served the bar.

In November 1982, she finally received the opportunity to perform for Wheel creator Merv Gryphon, which would forever alter her life. On the eve of Thanksgiving, she got employed. White said, "I was so anxious because I wanted this job so badly." "My mouth was trembling, my knees were trembling, and I could hardly speak."

3. "T" was White's initial letter on the wheel.

Before 1997, White had to manually rotate the puzzle wall's tiles as participants correctly identified the letters. She merely needs to touch the board to show the proper letters because the board is now computerised.

A week's worth of shows may be recorded in a single day thanks to computerization, which also makes it possible for the board to be updated more rapidly.

White is provided with the answers to the puzzles in advance so that she is aware of the locations of the letters to complete the task correctly. Nevertheless, she once added the incorrect letter to a puzzle, causing it to be thrown away.

4. White has only worn one outfit twice.

White has worn more than 7,000 different outfits over her career on the program, according to her home page on the Wheel of Fortune website. In September 2020, she finally wore the same clothing twice after going nearly 40 years without doing so. For those who watch Wheel and are ever seeking fashion ideas, the show also has a Pinterest board devoted to White's attire.

5. White's clapping earned him a Guinness World Record.

White was recognized as the television history's most frequent clapper by the Guinness Book of World Records in 2013. Throughout her 32 seasons on the program, White is thought to have clapped more than 3.7 million times in support of the candidates. That is an average of 606 applauses for each episode. A revised estimate from 2022 indicated that she had received more than 4.5 million claps.

6. White enjoys crocheting.

When White isn't being filmed, she doesn't spend time in the studio. She frequently crochets in the cosmetics area and in between takes. She says, "I love creating handmade presents." "People just no longer practise it... It is very unique. Both of my children will always have the handmade baby blankets I used to bring them home from the hospital.

7. White was in Playboy and filed a lawsuit.

When White was highlighted in Playboy magazine's May 1987 edition, a lot of admirers were astonished. The interior spread showed White seminude in provocative positions, and she appeared on the cover wearing only a long-sleeve shirt, according to The Washington Post.

White did not, however, appear in the magazine; instead, Hugh Hefner later acquired the 1982 images.

After that, White sued Playboy for $5.2 million and Hefner in federal court, alleging that the photographs would damage her reputation. However, White abandoned both lawsuits later that year.

During an appearance on The Tonight Show Starring Johnny Carson, she also made a public apology.

8. White makes money playing slots.

White is thought to have a net worth of about $85 million and receives a Wheel salary of over $10 million. However, White reportedly earns around $15 million extra a year, according to Brian Warner of Celebrity Net Worth, by licensing her name and likeness for slot machines.

There were 250 variations of the Wheel slot machine in circulation as of 2022, and since its introduction in 1996, they had paid out more than $3.3 billion.

9. She has appeared in several TV cameos

Despite having a difficult acting career previous to Wheel, White has used her work on the show to land several guest spots on scripted TV shows. She most recently had an appearance as herself on the ABC comedy Fresh Off the Boat in 2017, according to IMDb. On episodes of The A-Team, 227, L.A. Law, Full House, Just Shoot Me!, Married... with Children, and The King of Queens, she has also appeared in cameos.

Before she achieved fame, White took part in another popular game program. On June 20, 1980, she appeared on participants' row during an episode of The Price Is Right.

10. White enjoys helping others.

White is playing for the St. Jude Children's Research Hospital on Wednesday's "Ultimate Host" edition of Wheel, which is no accident. She has previously raised money for the organisation.

White, who enjoys crocheting, decided to use her pastime to do good by developing her yarn brand via Lion Brand, named "Vanna's Choice." As of

April 2019, she had contributed to St. Jude half of the earnings, raising over $2 million.

White stated of St. Jude, "Growing up in the South, it reminds me of my roots." "Many members of my family have battled cancer, including my mother, who passed away from it. I'm lucky to have two healthy children. And I'm pleased to contribute in any little way to St. Jude's efforts to help kids stay healthy.

How 'Wheel of Fortune' Helped Vanna White Cope With Personal Tragedies

As the hostess of the game program Wheel of Fortune for almost forty years, Vanna White has been disclosing letters, always with a grin.

That grin, however, has frequently concealed the television personality's suffering during her more than three decades on the program, particularly in her formative years when she tragically lost her fiancé in an accident.

White recalled the date to People magazine as May 17, 1986. "As soon as I learned about it, I knelt. Simply put, it was heartbreaking.

All of the pieces had been falling into place for the South Carolina native who had become a model. She had spent years working as a struggling actor, getting tiny parts in films like Graduation Day and Gipsy Angel in the 1980s and 1981s. In 1982, she beat out 200 other hopefuls to take over Susan Stafford's letter-turning responsibilities.

According to White, who is now a prominent writer, "They narrowed it down to me and one other girl, who just so happened to be a very good friend of mine." The day before Thanksgiving in 1982, when I learned I had won, was among the happiest of my life. I was relaxing in my flat when I unexpectedly received a call. I believe I yelled aloud.

She said that the show's inventor Merv Gryphon described her immediate chemistry with presenter Pat Sajak as having "brotherly and sisterly chemistry," which contributed to the Wheel of Fortune's enormous popularity.

The show had 30 million viewers in 1986, which was twice as many as the next highest-rated syndicated program, M*A*S*H, and was earning $100 million annually. In addition, she was preparing to wed her longtime lover Josh Gibson, a stripper, carpenter, sculptor, and actor on The Young and the Restless, the same year.

But when Gibson's single-engine Trinidad TB20, made in France, crashed on the last approach to Van Nuys Airport in the San Fernando Valley, all she had known fell apart. He passed away.

When this horrible event occurred, I was in the height of Vanna-mania, she recalled to Closer Weekly in 2018.

It was difficult to reconcile White's professional achievement with personal grief, but fortunately, there was a group of individuals willing to support White through his difficult time: Wheel of Fortune enthusiasts.

"I heard from so many people who had shared the same experience of losing someone instantly in an accident, and that helped me," she said, according to others. When something like that occurs, you instantly believe you are the only one. But I didn't feel alone.

The love I received from my followers, she continued, "was so incredible that it made me feel like I wasn't alone."

The unfathomable news came as an unbearable blow, but White eventually began to put herself back together with the support of her followers.

White married restaurateur George Santo Pietro in 1990, and 1992 she joyfully announced her pregnancy.

She pulled it off in a way that only a seasoned Wheel of Fortune hostess could, using a riddle that revealed "Vanna's Pregnant."

She remarked, "I so wanted to get pregnant and have a baby. So when I became pregnant, I wanted to announce it to everyone right away.

She experienced a miscarriage a week later. "I lost the baby, which was devastating after announcing it," White recalls. "Losing a child—there's nothing good about that."

She sought out her support network once more to endure the suffering. "You need to accept their help and make an effort to be resilient. Even if it's difficult, you must ask yourself, "What would they want me to do?" I've always had a close personal relationship with God and am a Christian. I pray but I don't preach about it since everyone has a right to their own beliefs. Every day, I pray.

And at the end of the tunnel, there was light. The mother of son Niko, born in 1994, and daughter Gigi, born in 1997, stated, "The good news is that I was able to get pregnant again and had two beautiful, healthy children." In 2002, Pietro and White got divorced.

White has persevered despite challenges to reach new milestones; on May 10, 2019, she shot the 7,000th episode of Wheel of Fortune, earning her a star on the Hollywood Walk of Fame in April 2006.

She was also given a place in the Guinness Book of World Records for the most applause, with 28,000 claps in a season and an average of 600 applause every show.

Her Wheel of Fortune team has been by her side the entire time. She claims, "We're one big family." "It's fantastic,"

The 11 Hidden Truths of Wheel Of Fortune

"Wheel of Fortune" Everyone is familiar with the well-known chant that opens each episode of the venerable game show. Wheel of Fortune has been on television for more than 40 years and is still going strong. Over the years, it has undergone a lot of alterations, and many mysteries are hidden beneath those rotating letters.

Learn how a little daytime game show became a national craze, spawned careers, and evolved into the primetime staple it is today.

1. The first Wheel of Fortune was much different.

Wheel of Fortune's original design was very different from what we see today. A game show centred on common people who performed heroic actions or little acts of bravery made its debut on CBS in 1952.

These people would appear on the program, tell their tale to America, and then spin the wheel to win a prize. The program's theme music, the popular song "Wheel of Fortune" by Kay Starr, survived the show's brief existence of roughly a year.

Todd Russell, who also hosts the kid-friendly puppet show The Rootie Kazootie Show, exceeds this Wheel of Fortune. Despite his lack of success in game shows, Russell was a pioneer in the vast field of spooky puppet child programs in the 1950s.

2. Shopper's Bazaar was the original name.

Why don't game shows include more shopping segments? The network had that opinion when a new Wheel of Fortune first began development in 1973. Because participants would frequently spend their prizes to buy, the show's initial name was supposed to be Shopper's Bazaar.

To be clear, unlike The Price is Right, shopping did not contribute to winning extra cash. The players played the game to win a Pontiac Firebird or an Indian squash blossom necklace after shopping for anything they wanted to win.

Wheel of Fortune continued to use the shopping theme for a time even if the name didn't make it past the pilot stage. The winner of the game, which was essentially the same as it is now, would have the opportunity to go on a little shopping extravaganza with their winnings. They may purchase items like oak patio furniture or a "Mahogany fun tub for two." Even though the shopping segment is now only a distant memory, it persisted until 1989, when producers realised it isn't very amusing to watch someone build a list of items they'd want to buy.

3. Susan Stafford and Chuck Woolery served as the initial hosts.

It's very unsettling to consider a Wheel of Fortune without Pat Sajak and Vanna White, but it occurred. Sajak and White weren't the show's first picks; in fact, Love Connection presenter Chuck Woolery initially spun the wheel and conducted interviews with contenders.

Even though Wheel began as a daytime show, they continued to give away prizes at primetime, including once giving away a Mercedes and even a little aeroplane, as Woolery subsequently remembered. Woolery gave the producer Merv Griffin's wage dispute as the reason he quit the program in 1981, although looking back, he believes he could have stayed a little bit longer.

Susan Stafford was there to wear the outfits and rotate the letters before White had touched a vowel. As she told the Chicago Tribune, "I mean, for seven years I stood there and turned letters."

She continued playing the game until she ultimately got bored. When asked if she regretted leaving in 1982, she responded, "Do I kick myself? No, I'm too proud of myself for that. Do I long for the cash? I do.

4. Susan Stafford departed the program to assist cancer sufferers.

In the months before her departure, Stafford had a deep-seated dissatisfaction with Wheel of Fortune. She told the Tribune that when she considered her life and work as the top letter changer, "I had to ask myself if that was any way for a grown woman to live her life."

She relocated to Houston to deal with cancer patients instead of attempting to get another acting role or continuing her modelling career.

Susan Stafford describes telling her supervisor she was quitting in her book Stop the Wheel, I Want to Get Off!, and how he responded, "Susan, you can't be serious. Even you would find this difficult. Later, she supposedly assisted Rock Hudson in finding Jesus on his deathbed after becoming a born-again Christian.

5. Pat Sajak wasn't wanted by the network

Wheel of Fortune's instigator Once Woolery quit the program, Merv Gryphon was left with the duty of choosing a replacement, and according to his book Making a Good Life Last, he wanted Pat Sajak from the beginning.

Gryphon admired Sajak, a weatherman at a nearby news station, for his sense of humour. Unfortunately, the network disagreed, particularly the head of daytime, who didn't think Sajak was capable of doing the job.

The network wasn't about to let a successful show slip away, so Sajak took up hosting responsibilities, striking a blow for justice on behalf of weathermen worldwide. Undaunted, Gryphon vowed to cease recording unless Sajak was recruited.

6. Vanna White caused a craze.
Vanna White's fame grew alongside Wheel of Fortune's, which is difficult to comprehend for

someone who primarily stands, grins, and spins things. With more than 30 million viewers, the program became the most-watched syndicated series of all time in 1986.

When "Vannamania" was in full swing in 1987, White made an appearance on the cover of Newsweek. The co-host received a tonne of fan mail and media coverage, and she became so well-liked that people began naming their children after her. When she joined the program in 1982, "Vanna" was the 8718th most common girl's name in the U.S. By the following year, its position had risen by more than 5,000 spots.

Vanna White began a clothing line and published a book after becoming famous; according to a poll of 90 percent of females, White was the ideal role model in 1986.

7. Pat and Vanna used to drink alcohol before recording

Sajak has acknowledged that even though he and White gave off the impression of being model citizens, they weren't always well-behaved. In an interview with ESPN2, Sajak revealed that he and White used to get wasted before tapings "when I first started and was much younger and could tolerate those things," adding, "We had a different show then."

He continued by saying that during their lengthy dinner breaks, they would go out and have a beautiful Mexican meal and several margaritas. Although Sajak stated he wouldn't mind seeing some of those old broadcasts to reminisce about the good ol' days when drinking on the job was completely OK, the days of the inebriated Wheel are long gone.

8. The Olympic torch was borne by Sajak and Vanna.

Sajak and White were chosen to carry the Olympic torch during the Summer Olympics in Atlanta in 1996 because they had been so deeply embedded in American popular culture. "Community and Local Heroes" carried the torch as it travelled over the majority of the nation, with the sporadic appearance of well-known people. Sajak and White had to pay $3,000 apiece for their moment with the torch, even though they were renowned enough to receive an Olympic invitation.

9. Vanna White has an international record.

As of 2017, Vanna White has been a letter-turning participant on Wheel of Fortune for close to 35 years, during which time she has donned more than 6500 outfits. She's never worn the same gown twice. Never the same one twice, she remarked in an interview with Fox (reported by Refinery29).

I'm not even allowed to retain them. They must return to the creator...I've tried on all the major trends, including those with large shoulder pads. I've completed just about anything. White favours something more elastic and comfy than anything else after wearing so many dresses; as she said, it's not much fun filming in a tight dress and five-inch heels.

White isn't complaining, of course; the program only shoots four days a month, and she is aware that some little garment discomfort is to be expected.

However, White's greatest accomplishment is even more specialised and has nothing to do with garments. She broke the Most Frequent Clapper Guinness World Record in 2013, a record we predict she will keep forever.

10. Merv Gryphon learned how difficult it was to replace Sajak.

Wheel's nightly leadership has been held by Pat Sajak for decades, however, he did step down from that position for a while. Producer Merv Gryphon relieved Sajak of his daytime hosting duties in 1990 while he was filming his brief-lived nighttime talk show The Pat Sajak Show, replacing him with former San Diego Chargers kicker Rolf Benirschke, who admitted he had never watched the show and didn't understand how the game was played.

Benirschke seems unfazed by being dismissed and shrugged, saying, "I didn't seek this to begin with. I liked it, and while I would consider other things, I won't pursue them. I value my way of life in San Diego far too highly.

Gryphon hired veteran game show presenter and sportscaster Bob Goen after Benirschke was fired, but despite Goen's skills, the show failed. When reflecting on his experience, Goen said in an interview, "We were the poor stepsister to the nighttime syndicated version with Pat and Vanna.

While we were struggling with $50 wheel spacing and gave out GEO Metros, they were making millions and giving away BMWs. It was a little embarrassing and, in my opinion, the final straw for my version of the program. In 1991, the midday Wheel was no longer shown.

11. It has competed with Jeopardy for viewers.

For years, Jeopardy! and Wheel of Fortune have competed for the top spot in syndicated ratings. Wheel frequently triumphs, but Jeopardy! still makes an effort. Jeopardy! has occasionally won in previous years, but as of March 2017, Wheel has reclaimed the top spot, albeit only by a slim margin.

Since they have been TV mainstays for so long, both shows are performing exceptionally well; in fact, it is unusual for either show to finish lower than sixth among all nationally syndicated programming. That's outstanding for something that has been broadcast for more than 40 years.

Made in the USA
Monee, IL
06 January 2025

76180206R00030